Seasons in the Garden

APRIL

Spring bulbs, especially daffodils; flowering shrubs; some rhododendrons; camellias (under glass).

MAY

Bulbs, especially tulips and bluebells; primulas; *Meconopsis*; flowering shrubs including *Prunus*, *Pyrus*, rhododendrons and azaleas.

JUNE

Border flowers including lupins, irises and lilies; primulas; *Meconopsis*; peonies; roses; flowering shrubs including *Philadelphus*, rhododendrons and azaleas.

JULY

Orangery Borders; peonies; primulas; water lilies (outside); kniphofias; roses.

AUGUST

Orangery Borders; dahlias; primulas; roses.

SEPTEMBER

Border flowers including asters, heleniums and dahlias; autumn bulbs; roses; autumn foliage and berries on the trees, especially maples, *Sorbus* and *Malus*

OCTOBER

Border flowers especially asters; autumn bulbs; autumn foliage and berries.

CONTENTS & MAP OF GARDEN

Key to Map

1 ARCHWAY LEADING TO HOUSE ENTRANCE
2 LODGE
3 ORANGERY SHOP & HOUSE EXIT
4 LAVATORIES
5 REFRESHMENTS
6 LAVATORIES, DISABLED LAVATORIES,
   BABY ROOM, COACH DRIVERS
   REST ROOM & TELEPHONE
7 REFRESHMENTS & INFORMATION
8 GARDEN ENTRANCE & EXIT
9 POTTING SHED GARDEN SALES
10 LAVATORIES & TELEPHONE
11 CARRIAGE HOUSE RESTAURANT
12 CARRIAGE HOUSE SHOP

Rhododendrons

Morton Pond

Arboretum

Spectacles

Cascade House

Cottage Garden

Kitchen Garden

12

11

The Cascade House

The Maze

Blanche's Vase

The Serpentine Hedge

The Squirting Willow Tree Fountain

Looking South over the Seahorse Fountain and Canal Pond

The Conservative Wall

The Cottage Garden

Grotto Pond

Ravine

Azalea Dell

Hundred Steps

Old Conservatory Garden and Maze

Bust of 6th Duke

Blanche's Vase

War Horse

Wellington Rock

Serpentine Hedge

Canal Pond

Rockeries

The Strid

Ring Pond

Willow Tree Fountain

Cascade

Emperor Fountain

Salisbury Lawns

Broad Walk

South Lawn

Sea-horse Fountain

Rose Garden

Display Greenhouse

Flora's Temple

S
E ← → *W*
N

8

3

5

4

8

7

6

2

1

THE WEST GARDEN
(Private)

This is not open to visitors but is seen from the window of the State Dressing Room on the tour of the house

The architectural parterres designed by Wyatville for the 6th Duke used to be filled with bedded-out plants, never very satisfactory, and I am much more pleased with the new scheme of sharp geometrical patterns of box which fit very well with the old golden yew cushions at each corner and a new clipped yew in the middle.

Parterre *c.* 1830 by Sir Jeffrey Wyatville, planted with box

The garden is long and narrow and makes a funnel for the north wind, so my husband decided to cut it into three with yew hedges. The middle division was a problem. It is important, because all the west windows of the house look down on it.

There was a wretched muddle of shrubs in the four corners, a motley collection of a specially unattractive pink prunus, junipers and cupressus. Inspiration for this place came in 1960 when I was looking at an exhibition of the architectural plans of Chiswick House, Lord Burlington's perfect little palace on the outskirts of London. It struck me that the circle of the dome was about the same size as the round pond, and from then on it was simple. We copied the plan of walls, stairs and pillars, and it is only one foot out of scale. It was planted in golden box, 3,350 of them, golden because the dark climate of Derbyshire needs any brightening it can get.

Design in golden box copied from the ground-plan of Chiswick House, London

When they were ordered the nurseryman said, 'No one has wanted *that* since 1914'. The design must be looked down on from above. It is meaningless, except for children to steeplechase over, when you are on its own level.

THE ORANGERY BORDERS AND THE BROAD WALK

Having gone round the house you go out into the garden from the Orangery (now a shop). Visitors who come only to the garden enter through Flora's Temple – the high building with pillars in the garden wall – or by the entrance at the corner of the Stables.

Marble statue of Flora attributed to Caius Gabriel Cibber (1630–1700)

The Orangery was built in 1827 to house the 6th Duke's plants. Here, on either side of the path, the borders are planted entirely with blue and white annuals, herbaceous plants and 'Iceberg' roses, backed by clipped and bound Irish Yews (*Taxus baccata* 'Fastigiata'), while the borders across the Broad Walk, backed by hard-pruned red oaks (*Quercus rubra*), are similarly planted but in yellow, orange and red. The stone dogs each side of the steps above the orange and red border are copies of the Molossian Hound, or Dog of Alcibiades, a classical sculpture formerly at Duncombe Park, Yorkshire.

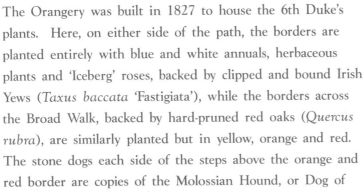

The Broad Walk with a view of Flora's Temple (extreme left), the *Conservative Wall*, the Stables (designed by James Paine and completed in 1763) and, on the hill above, Stand Wood with the Hunting Tower (*c.* 1582) at its summit

Flora's Temple was built in 1695 by the 1st Duke of Devonshire as a bowling-green house, designed in imitation of a classical temple. Originally it was situated a quarter of a mile away in what is now the private garden; it was rebuilt in its present position in about 1760. Flora herself, probably carved by Caius Gabriel Cibber (1630–1700), has moved several times. Originally the centre-piece of "Flora's Garden", an area laid out by the 1st Duke in the 1690s to the south of the house, she was moved *c.* 1765 into the former Bowling Green House, which thus became Flora's Temple. In 1813 she was next set up by the 6th Duke in his new French Garden, now the Rose Garden, but in 1993 she returned to her Temple after being cleaned and restored.

By Flora's Temple is a limestone boulder deposited nearly a quarter of a million years ago by a glacier moving south from Pindale near Castleton. Another curiosity here is the cheese press brought from the cellar of a cottage in Edensor in 1950.

Left:
Flora's Temple

Right:
Detail from engraved perspective view by Kip & Knyff, 1699. Lower left is the Bowling Green House, which later became Flora's Temple. Lower right is Flora's Garden with Flora at its centre

6

The Broad Walk

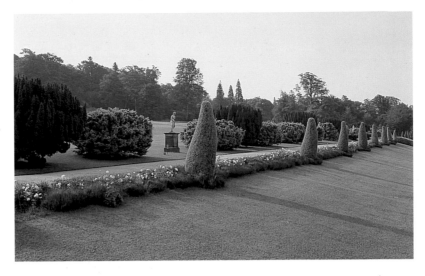

The Broad Walk of the 1820s, *'Wyatville's first great hit out of doors'*, as the 6th Duke called it, is a third of a mile long. It runs south from Flora's Temple parallel to the east front of the house past the Orangery, Sculpture Gallery, Great Dining Room, Ante Library and Library, with the kitchens and other offices below and the Leicester and Wellington bedrooms above. The path continues between the Salisbury Lawns and the South Lawn and on through a beech avenue ending at the top of a rise with Blanche's Vase on the skyline. The vase was commissioned by the 6th Duke in memory of his beloved niece.

The Broad Walk
looking south to
Blanche's Vase

The row of yews, golden (*Taxus baccata* 'Aureomarginata') and green (*Taxus baccata* 'Fastigiata'), along the Broad Walk, replaced monkey puzzle trees about 100 years ago. Note how much stronger are those sheltered by the house from the west wind.

Blanche's Vase

THE CONSERVATIVE WALL

The 'Conservative Wall' (as Paxton called it, because it conserves heat), glazed by him in 1848, runs up the hillside from Flora's Temple to the stables in a series of ascending steps 331 feet long. It contains figs, peaches, nectarines and apricots as well as shrubs such as *Chimonanthus praecox* and *Buddleia auriculata* which would not live out of doors in our harsh climate. In the high central portion are two *Camellia reticulata* 'Captain Rawes' planted about 1850. In March and April they are covered in huge pink flowers with wavy petals and gold stamens. Their trunks are 2ft 6ins in circumference at 3ft high. The tree peonies flanking the steps were given to us by the gamekeeper from his garden in Pilsley in about 1955. Opposite, over the steps, is a laburnum tunnel planted in 1974.

and the Snake Terrace

The Camellia
Reticulata in the
Conservative
Wall

The Snake Terrace and the one above it were constructed in 1974, four years after the Display Greenhouse was built. Till then there was a shrubbery here of no interest and lean-to sheds against the north side of the 1st Duke's Greenhouse. We left the holly and the yew which were part of the shrubbery and made the brick terrace round them. The paving stones making the circle were salvaged from Paxton's Lily House (1850) in the old kitchen garden. There they formed the rim of the first *Victoria amazonica* lily pond. The bricks were kilned at Chatsworth c. 1840. The snake (the family crest) is made of pebbles from the Crumbles beach at Eastbourne. The cushion on which it rests is black Ashford and red Alport marbles from nearby quarries. It was designed by Dennis Fisher (Comptroller 1962-1979) and constructed by Malcolm Sellors of Bakewell.

The star of pebbles surrounded by a brick floor was copied from the garden of a friend in Oxfordshire. The enclosing walls are built of stone which was the base of the old orchid houses next to the existing vine house. These stones were sawn in halves thus doubling the quantity and revealing new surfaces and the beautiful grain of this local sandstone.

9

THE DISPLAY GREENHOUSE

The Display Greenhouse (built in 1970) has three climates: tropical, Mediterranean and temperate. There is a pool in the tropical section made for the *Victoria amazonica* lily. This astonishing plant is a perennial, but is grown as an annual in temperate latitudes. As the days lengthen so the leaves reach their full size; giant green saucers with upturned rims. Paxton brought the lily from Kew, where it had failed to flower, in 1849 and persuaded it to flower for the first time in this country at Chatsworth in the same year. Pawpaw (*Carica papaya*) thrives and fruits in this section of the house; so does the banana (*Musa* 'Cavendishii') which fruits well. This small, sweet banana was originally imported in 1829 and did so well at Chatsworth that Paxton sent one to an English missionary in Samoa where it flourished. It is now widely grown commercially, especially in the Canary Islands. Also growing here are *Stephanotis, Jasminum rex, Passiflora quadrangularis*, better known by its fruit granadilla and which, as the name suggests, has a square stem;

Pamianthe peruviana, gardenias, Dutchman's pipe (*Aristolochia brasiliensis*), the *Eucharis* lily, an unusual member of the daffodil family, a curious and sinister nearly black flower called *Tacca aspera*, the heavily scented frangipani (*Plumeria rubra*) and a mango (*Mangifera indica*).

In the middle section are oranges, lemons and limes as well as *Datura* species and the dramatic night-flowering cactus (*Selenicereus grandiflorus*) which comes from Jamaica. Sometimes it produces as many as 100 flowers 12 inches across. They open as darkness falls to attract the night-flying insects that pollinate them. In the morning they are all dead, hanging like damp socks and giving no idea of their midnight beauty. A Black Hamburgh vine grows up the arches in the middle. In the temperate section are camellias, tender rhododendrons like 'Fragrantissimum', a white-heart cherry and an apricot, which would not fruit outside, *Lapageria rosea* (the national flower of Chile) and *Mahonia lomariifolia* (spectacular yellow flowers in November). The ground cover is sorrel for early spring soup. There is an arch of fuchsias here. The engineering complexities of this greenhouse are beyond my ken but there are descriptive notices concerning them on the doors.

THE 1ST DUKE'S GREENHOUSE
AND THE ROSE GARDEN

The rather conventional rose garden, planted mostly with Hybrid Teas underplanted with pansies and mallows, is bordered by a yew hedge with the 1st Duke's Greenhouse (1698) at the north side. The purchase of oranges and myrtles shown in the accounts for that year must have been for this greenhouse. Now it contains some of the big collection of camellias and other half-hardy plants like mimosa and *Lapageria rosea*. The camellias are usually among the prize winners at the Royal Horticultural Society Spring Show and one, *C. japonica* 'Mathotiana rubra' is acknowledged to be outstanding. It has blood red, almost purple flowers. Some of the bigger camellias came from Ditchley Park, Oxfordshire, a present from Ronald Tree when he sold that extraordinarily beautiful place in the 1950s. Along the front of the greenhouse there are box-edged divisions planted with irises and standard gooseberries. The yews at each end are smothered by the climbing and rambling roses 'Bobbie James', 'Wedding Day', 'Kiftsgate', 'Paul's Himalayan Musk', and *Rosa filipes*.

11

Left:
View through the 1st Duke's Greenhouse
looking south to the Serpentine Hedge

George Pearce, the architect of the Display
House, noticed the archway in the wall of the
1st Duke's Greenhouse and suggested it should
be opened up. This was done and gives a view
across the Salisbury Lawns, the Ring Pond and
up the serpentine hedge of beech to the statue
of the 6th Duke, a third of a mile away.

Below: The 1st Duke's Greenhouse in its
original position in front of the former
Greenhouse Pond. Detail from engraved
perspective by Kip & Knyff, 1699

Left:
The Serpentine
Hedge in early
spring looking north
towards the 1st
Duke's Greenhouse

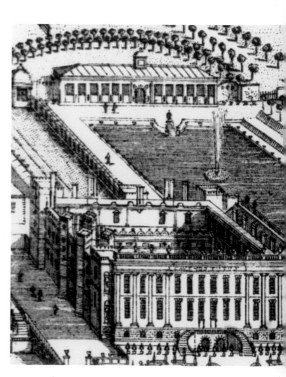

12

THE SALISBURY LAWNS

The Salisbury Lawns are worthy of special note. Working for the 4th Duke in the 1760s Lancelot 'Capability' Brown destroyed the formal terraces with their parterres and fountains to create three acres of grass, then called The Great Slope. This ground was smoothed and laid out as a lawn, not only filling the whole background of the house but stretching far on either side beyond it. The bills for ploughing, laying it down to grass, the hay seeds with which it was planted, rolling and harrowing, are all in the account book of 1755-65. Since that time little or nothing has been done to change it and I am sure it offends people who like a billiard-table green lawn with no weeds. But since the fashion is now all for wild flowers perhaps it pleases more than it offends, as heather, yarrow, knapweed, ox-eye daisy, lady's bedstraw, mouse-ear hawkweed, cat's ear, birdsfoot trefoil, sorrel, white clover, speedwell, tormentil, harebell, milkwort, dandelion, creeping buttercup, plantain and even the yellow mountain pansy as well as the usual grasses and plenty of moss grow on the lawns. These were all identified by Dr. O. L. Gilbert of Sheffield University when he made a study of the lawns in 1983.

When first laid down the grass was close-cropped by deer. It has been mown, except in wartime, ever since the deer were excluded from this part of the garden early in the 19th century.

There are some damp patches covered in a slimy algal growth which is dangerously slippery and has caused many a fall. Please beware of this hazard.

13

Myself, I greatly regret that the 4th Duke engaged Brown to make such drastic changes in the 1st Duke's formal garden and would dearly love to see the terraces, parterres and waterworks as they were in the early 1700s. In his passion for the 'natural' it is a mercy that he spared the Cascade. However, I think his treatment of the park is peerless. The view to the west is worth pausing to take in. The trees on the distant hill which form the rim of the park were planted by Brown. He arranged them in wedge-shaped plantings so that when one section is felled there is another to take its place, thereby ensuring an unchanging skyline. The apparently natural clumps of trees elsewhere in the 1000-acre park are typical of his work. Brown was a master at planning landscapes on the grand scale, and there is hardly a county in England where his genius is not evident.

One of a series of 9 stone statues after the Antique, at the foot of the Salisbury Lawns, bordering the Broad Walk.
English, early 19th century

No telegraph poles or power lines
have been allowed on the park
roads, either public or private, to vex
the eye. So the view from the
Salisbury Lawns is virtually
unchanged since the 1760s except
that we see some of the trees in
their mature beauty.

Enclosed in a low white fence is our
weather station where the rainfall
and sunshine are recorded daily.
The average annual rainfall is about
33.7 inches and the sunshine 1,160
hours.

THE CASCADE

The Cascade was built for the 1st Duke. Finished in 1696 it was rebuilt only five years later on a grander scale. It was designed by a Frenchman, Grillet, a pupil of the celebrated Le Nôtre. The Temple or Cascade House was added in 1703 to the plans of Thomas Archer, the Warwickshire architect. The carving in stone on the building is by Nadauld and Samuel Watson. The length of the paving stones over which the water flows and the numbers and widths of the 24 groups of steps are all different so the sound of the falling water varies. At the base of the Cascade the water disappears underground, passes through a pipe and works the Sea-horse Fountain on the South Lawn in front of the house, goes underground again to work the fountain in the West Garden below the house, and finally is piped into the river. The Cascade was taken up and relaid by the 6th Duke *c.* 1830 when he discovered it was slightly out of line with the new gravel path he had built up the slope.

Repointing the Cascade each year after frost damage became such a problem that the only solution was to rebuild it. During three winters 1994–96 all 24 bays were taken up and rebuilt using the original stone where possible and new local matching stone where not.

Looking west down the Cascade

The new stone was dressed using the original techniques and for the last 13 bays took one mason 1,200 hours to prepare. The entire job took 10,000 man hours, 55 tonnes of sand, 45 tonnes of concrete and 54 tonnes (42 cubic metres) of new stone.

Archer's Cascade House with its statues, dolphins and "frost-worke", was cleaned and repointed. The decayed stonework was rebuilt including the stepped dome. All the lead was replaced and the waterpipes on the roof of the facade restored to their full effect. A continuous flow over the dome, however, would use up too much water, so it is kept for special occasions.

The Cascade during restoration, 1995–96

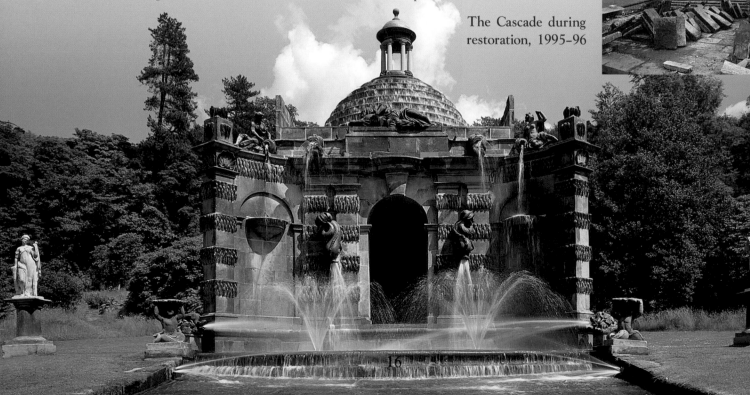

The water for the Cascade and the Emperor Fountain is supplied by natural pressure from four large reservoir lakes, all man-made, on the plateau above the wood. They in turn are fed from miles of conduits which drain the moor. The waterworks are turned on only when the garden is open to visitors and in a

The pool at the head of the Cascade

Cascade House dome before and during restoration

Right: Part of the Emperor Lake, one of four man-made reservoirs that feed the fountains

dry summer the hours they play have to be rationed as the water is not re-cycled. Under the Cascade half-way down is a dark and damp tunnel. The 6th Duke's *Handbook* (1844) says '*The Cascade is old, the tunnel underneath it the newest of the new, contrived to hide the march of coal carts conveying fuel to the Great Conservatory*' (p22) The Cascade House and its watery forecourt contain a series of fountains and jets from which the Cascade is fed. Even the dome of the House can be turned into a waterfall, and the floor of the interior is pierced by holes with jets to soak the surprised visitor. It is worth climbing up to the Cascade House to see the whole length (208 yards) of the steep watered stairs running down the hill, the Salisbury Lawns, the house, across the river Derwent to the hills of the park to the west, farmland and woods above, with Edensor church spire (1867) by Sir George Gilbert Scott dominating the village in its own little valley.

An avenue of limes (*Tilia platyphyllos* 'Rubra') was planted in 1985 to define the edge of the lawn bordering the Cascade and the woodland garden.

THE WILLOW TREE FOUNTAIN

'There . . . in the middle of ye grove stands a fine willow tree, the leaves, barke and all looks very naturall, ye roote is full of rubbish or great stones to appearance and all on a sudden by turning a sluce it raines from each leafe and from the branches like a shower, it being made of brass and pipes to each leafe, but in appearance is exactly like any willow.'

Extract from the diary of Celia Fiennes, who visited Chatsworth in 1696

Turn left off the main path below the Cascade and you will find the Willow Tree Fountain which was first 'planted' in its own secluded little dell in 1692. The original 'tree' was made of copper and lead. It spurts water from its branches and leaves, and in winter it looks so much like the other leafless trees that its trick of wetting the unwary is all the more surprising. This 'squirting tree' delighted Princess Victoria when she came to Chatsworth aged 13. It has been replaced twice and was last restored in 1983. The pond which is the reservoir for this curiosity is near the top of the Cascade. A lead statue of Pan which for many years had lain broken was restored in 1991 and returned to its plinth behind the Willow Tree Fountain.

18

THE ROCKERIES

Passing under a precarious-looking arch of massive rocks you will see the 'Rocking Stone' now firmly fixed in the middle of the path. Lord Desart writing in the 1860s describes it thus *'In one place a sort of miniature Matterhorn apparently blocked the path but with a touch of the finger it revolved upon a metal axis and made a way to pass'*.

Nancie Park and the Rocking Stone,
photographed in 1985

During the 1939-45 war the girls of Penrhos College occupied Chatsworth and Nancie Park, a pupil at the school, describes the Stone in her book *School Days at Chatsworth*, *'At the narrow entrance to this copper tree there was a vast stone which, when pushed, went slowly round like a revolving door in a hotel. One day, in a rush of enthusiasm and probably showing off, I crushed my right leg between the moving stone and the entrance. I duly suffered. I was in bed for a week and the bruising was most impressive. The stone was immediately wedged, making it non-mobile, but we still refer to it as the rolling stone'*.

In the autumn of 1842' wrote the 6th Duke *'there was not a single stone in these parts; you will now find a labyrinth of rocky walks. You would be surprised to see the structure of which the foundations were then laid. I charge you to take notice of several features of this new work; of the old copper willow tree re-appearing after a long eclipse, the* Queen's Rock, Prince Albert's and the Duke of Wellington's last removed and grandest of all. The spirit of some Druid seems to animate Mr. Paxton in these bulky removals.' Such huge boulders piled on top of one another are a far cry from most people's idea of a rock garden. They become more dramatic as you walk on.

Both the challenge of the physical difficulty of moving rocks weighing several tons and the happy result of the way they fit their surroundings, looking as if they occur naturally in the landscape, appealed to Paxton. His *'bulky removals'* have become one of the most intriguing parts of the garden. He wisely decided they should be *'some distance from the mansion'* and advises that *'all the vegetation which accompanies an extensive rockery should be subordinate to it . . . and be merely sufficient and so disposed as to give relief and diversity to it'*.

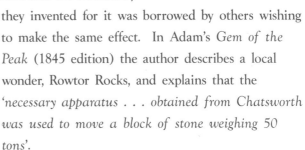

So adept did Paxton and his men become at their task that the machinery they invented for it was borrowed by others wishing to make the same effect. In Adam's *Gem of the Peak* (1845 edition) the author describes a local wonder, Rowtor Rocks, and explains that the *'necessary apparatus . . . obtained from Chatsworth was used to move a block of stone weighing 50 tons'*.

After Paxton and his patron died fashion changed and nature was encouraged to hide as much of the rockeries as possible. Yews were allowed to grow and blot out their forms; shrubs and climbers masked the stone, ivy and other evergreens made green mounds out of Paxton's bare rocks.

We are clearing some of it now and I hope this part of the garden will soon look as Paxton intended: *'The most picturesque assemblage of natural rocks'*.

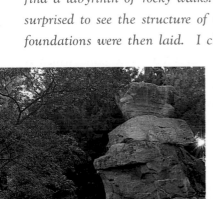

THE WELLINGTON ROCK

The grandest rock of them all is the Wellington. It is 45 feet high and over it a waterfall drops into its own little pond. The waterfall looks natural but, like so much in the garden, it is not. The Rock is made up of many big stones cemented together and the water is piped from a stream above. The whole affair is like a giant out-of-doors stage set. At the base of the Rock are some large clumps of *Gunnera manicata* (from Southern Brazil).

Their vast rhubarb-like leaves grow with surprising speed in the spring and in the winter their roots are covered with their own dead leaves, topped up with bracken, to protect them from the frost. They, and the giant hogweed (*Heracleum mantegazzianum*) from the Caucasus, are of the right scale for this monumental 'rock garden'. Beware of touching the hogweed; it can produce a rash. Bamboos flourish here and edging the Wellington Rock pond are *Primula japonica* in early summer followed by *P. florindae* in July and August. *Aquilegia*, foxgloves, *Meconopsis* (the Himalayan blue poppy) and azaleas flower in May and June; various maples and some unusual pear trees (*Pyrus* 'Durondeau', 'Thompson's', 'Josephine de Malines' and 'Winter Nellis') are planted here. On the bank between the Queen's and Prince Albert's Rocks are several varieties of *Philadelphus* given to me by the Chesterfield, Buxton, Derby and Matlock committees of the Children's Society when I retired from their Presidencies in 1985.

The little stream, which reappears opposite the Wellington Rock after going under the path, runs through a conduit to make yet another waterfall into the Strid. This was created by Paxton and named after that stretch of the Wharfe near Bolton Abbey in Yorkshire where the broad river narrows into a chasm only a yard wide. The force of the water there is terrifying; although it is possible to jump it the attempt has often proved fatal. Here it is tame enough. There are trout in the Strid Pond, making rings in the water when they rise to take flies on summer evenings. There are some big *Rosa moyesii*, patches of colchicums and autumn crocus, *Rheum palmatum* and its variety 'Atrosanguineum', lace-cap and other hydrangeas round the pond. In 1985 a large planting of red-hot pokers (*Kniphofia*) was made among the rocks which make a striking show in early summer. The rampant climbing rose 'Bobbie James' grows over some of the yews. Suitably enough there is a large Wellingtonia (*Sequoiadendron giganteum*) on the lawn, its soft

AND THE STRID

bark unfortunately much buffeted by visitors. A magnificent sessile oak (*Quercus petraea*), with a bole to gladden the heart of a forester and make a joiner reach for his saw, stands at the mouth of a dark cave, the entrance (now blocked) to the underground tramway designed by Paxton to supply the coal to the eight huge boilers that heated his Great Conservatory (p. 22).

The Wellington Rock is a fine sight in a hard winter when the waterfall freezes after heavy rain and turns it into a curtain of ice – a complete contrast to the same place on a warm June day when the primulas are in flower and the flow of water is reduced to a trickle.

Three striking plants which are to be seen here have naturalised themselves and turn up all over the place. They are giant bellflower (*Campanula latifolia*), tall enough to look right in these surroundings and with flowers in all shades of blue; elecampane (*Inula helenium*) which grows to 5 feet and has a very big orange daisy-like flower, and several varieties of *Verbascum*. These send up spikes of yellow flowers from rosettes of leaves with a white and woolly look and grow in poor, stony places.

Brown Trout

THE OLD CONSERVATORY GARDEN

Having passed the Wellington Rock and the Strid continue along the wide path and you come to a high stone archway, the entrance to the site of the Great Conservatory built by Paxton and Decimus Burton in 1836-40. The building sprang from 3ft 6ins stone walls, now sadly all that is left of the famous greenhouse, but they give an idea of its size. The method of building was the culmination of years of experiments with glasshouses and the outcome of the happy combination of Paxton's flair for engineering and love of plants. Here he created an ideal indoor garden where all manner of exotics could be grown.

It covered just over three-quarters of an acre. The surface area of the roof was 52,287 sq. ft. and the 24,560 sash bars measured about 40 miles. The coal supply needed to heat the million cubic feet of air was dumped out of sight behind the Wellington Rock and transported thence by an underground tramway to the boilers beneath the building, which contained 7 miles of 4-inch hot water pipes.

When the Great Conservatory was finished it caused a sensation and people came from all over the world to marvel at '*a tropical scene with a glass sky*' as the King of Saxony described it. Queen Victoria drove through it in an open carriage when she stayed at Chatsworth in 1843. It was lit for the occasion by 12,000 lamps placed along the ribs. None of his garden buildings gave the 6th Duke more pleasure and he described the individual plants at length in his *Handbook*.

The Maze in the Conservatory Garden

Below: The Great Conservatory c. 1890

Below right: The Garden Staff c. 1890

The Great Conservatory existed for only 80 years. After the 1914-18 war the plants were dead as there were no men to look after them and no coal for heating. In 1920 the 9th Duke decided that it had to be pulled down; ironically it was Paxton's grandson, Charles Markham, who supervised the demolition work.

The demolition of the
Great Conservatory 1920

The Hundred Steps leading down
to the Old Conservatory Garden

23

The north end of the Old Conservatory Garden planted with
Michaelmas daisies and dahlias

The garden within the foundation walls of the
Old Conservatory has been used in various
ways in the last 70 years. Now the north end is
devoted to autumn flowers, dahlias and Michaelmas
daisies and the south end is all lupins. Mop-
headed acacias (*Robinia pseudoacacia*
'Inermis') are planted in the flower beds to give
height here and there. These lovely little trees
remain a light spring green till October. In the
middle section is a maze, planted in 1962
with 1,209 yews. The old yew hedges have
been allowed to grow to form two arches in the
middle, repeating in dark green the stone arches
at each end of this garden. Peonies are planted
round the outside of the foundation walls and
the big evergreen trees on the surrounding banks
are Wellingtonias (*Sequoiadendron giganteum*) and
Lawson cypress (*Chamaecyparis lawsoniana*).

Dahlias and
Michaelmas daisies

Lupins (above) in May and June,
autumn dahlias (left) and the ornamental vine
Ampelopsis (below)

25

THE GROTTO

Approaching the Grotto Pond from the green drive which encompasses the garden, or walking up from the old Conservatory Garden which joins this drive, you pass four big Japanese red cedars (*Cryptomeria japonica*) as the pond comes into view. These trees were introduced to England in 1842 and some were planted here soon afterwards. At the far (south east) corner of the pond is one of the tallest Weymouth pines (*Pinus strobus*) in England. It measured 121 feet high in 1983. The Grotto Pond is an ancient fish pond and marked the southernmost end of the garden till 1829 when the 6th Duke enclosed eight acres of parkland to make his pinetum. The 6th Duke wrote in 1844 'The grotto was built by my mother; and I respected its exterior when the addition was made of a natural cavern, formed of crystals of copper ore that were discovered in Ecton mine, on the borders of Staffordshire, and had to be removed in the hope of finding some of the lost side veins. Vain hope! the produce ceased to repay the labour of the works, instead of amounting, as it is said to have done in one year, to the sum of £300,000 - a fortunate God-send, that paid for the building of Buxton Crescent, and I should hope for a great deal besides. The crystals are curious, because they contain the ore, instead of being, as is usual, encrusted by it'. His mother was Lady Georgiana Spencer (1757-1806), the celebrated wife of the 5th Duke of Devonshire. Grottoes and hermitages and suchlike follies were fashionable in her time. In 1798 White Watson, the Bakewell geologist, was paid £66.18.9 for his 'time and trouble in designing the grotto and for fossils'. Georgiana was a collector of minerals and would have delighted in her son's addition of a cavern lined with shining copper crystals. It is now kept locked.

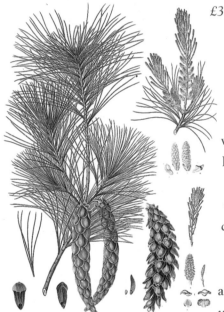

Foliage and cones of the Weymouth Pine (*Pinus strobus*). An illustration from *The Genus Pinus* by A. B. Lambert (London, 1828-37)

The roof of the Grotto was originally thatched. The 1820 account book notes, 'Sampson Newton was paid £12.5.6 for watching at night to prevent depradations'. There is no record of the date when the bandstand and its roof were added.

Being so far from the house it is a secluded place, so this quiet pond and its surroundings are a haven for birds and beasts and insects which live on or near water. Dippers, grebes and teal, as well as the commoner kinds of duck, come to feed. There are always wild pheasants here and a pair of woodcock nest in this part of the garden most years.

Some clearing has been done lately in this area and new trees and shrubs have been planted including a number of swamp cypresses (*Taxodium distichum*). These slow-growing trees turn a foxy red before shedding their needles in the autumn.

On the bank below the Grotto are several varieties of *Hamamelis*, brooms and willows. *Rosa filipes* grows up the big oak here and next to the Grotto itself is the skeleton of another ancient oak, more sculptural than arboreal. These oaks, and those in the Old Park beyond the garden wall, are relics of old Sherwood Forest. This bank is the only place in the garden where cowslips grow happily and seed themselves. Only the path is mown so there is a succession of wild flowers in the long grass, which is not cut till about the end of August. The steps by the rocks lead up to the 1920s plantings of rhododendrons, seedlings from one of Kingdon Ward's Himalayan expeditions to which the 9th Duke subscribed. Two tracks, impassable till the 1986 clearing, run parallel to the main grass path through part of the arboretum.

Autumn is often the most rewarding season in this part of the country so we are planting more shrubs which colour well such as liquidamber, many varieties of maples, *Cercidiphyllum*, *Sorbus* 'Joseph Rock', *S. vilmorinii* etc.

The pond has to be dredged from time to time as the plants of the great reed mace and other pond weeds encroach and would eventually cause it to silt up.

In 1986 an old track, overgrown and out of sight for years, was revealed. It runs from the north west corner of the pond above the Old Conservatory garden and peters out where the new steps have been made. I suppose it was obliterated by the spoil from the levelling of the ground for the Great Conservatory and other work. It is clearly marked on the map of 1773 and was an exciting discovery.

THE PINETUM
AND THE ARBORETUM

In 1829 the 6th Duke enclosed 8 acres of the park at the south end of the garden to make his Pinetum. Many of the conifers he planted were new introductions to this country. He was an enthusiastic collector of plants and sent expeditions all over the world to add to those available from nurserymen. He wrote in his *Handbook* '*This ground is a new addition from the park; it is much admired but no two of a party take the same views of it; one extols the scenery another is in raptures at the old oaks, and a third wonders and asks, why I plant the fir trees so thin? That is the Douglas Pine the pride of California: which came down in Mr. Paxton's hat in 1839, and in 1845 it is 35 feet high*'. Many were blown down in the gale of 1962 but some of the original plantings still to be seen are *Sequoiadendron giganteum* with its soft, spongy bark, *Pinus contorta, P. ponderosa, P. strobus, P. mugo, Juniperus chinensis, Pseudotsuga menziesii* and *Araucaria araucana* (monkey puzzle).

Most of the trees are labelled now but we have yet to discover the best way to do this. The 6th Duke's method was not ideal either. A Russian visitor thought the names of the trees painted on dark wooden boards *'appeared dismal to a romantic foreigner who exclaimed "Oh my God how touching! These are no doubt the tombs of the plants".'* (6th Duke's *Handbook*.)

Over 100 years passed with no change but in 1956 a few were added: *Abies veitchii, A. firma, Chamaecyparis pisifera* 'Squarrosa', *C. lawsoniana* 'Stewartii', *C. nootkatensis* 'Pendula', *Picea pungens* 'Globosa' and *Sequoia sempervirens*. In 1985 60 conifers were planted here and some *Sorbus vilmorinii,* valuable for their pale pink berries which cheer up a dark November day.

Joseph Paxton's Arboretum was planned (1835) as a systematic succession of trees in accordance with botanical classification. Few traces of this survive and what we call the Arboretum today are those parts of the garden where trees and shrubs are dominant. Much of this area has recently been cleared of an impenetrable mass of self-sown *Rhododendron ponticum*, sycamore, yew, laurel and holly. Paths were impassable and work done in the winters of 1985, 1986 and 1987 revealed places in the garden I had never seen; and I have lived here for over 40 years. To our astonishment a statue was discovered knocked from its plinth in a tangle of evergreens.

Above:
Rhododendrons

Left:
Bluebells in the
Arboretum

Following the broad path northwards from the Grotto you pass *'the tall larch which the old house-keeper's father remembered to have seen brought in a pot from Welbeck as a curiosity'* (Handbook, 1844). The recent clearing has revealed the boles of the trees, including some remarkable oaks below the garden wall to the east. We have opened a view down to the maze in the Old Conservatory Garden and 100 steps have been constructed. Descending the steps you can see the structure of the subterranean chimney which took the smoke from the furnaces of the Great Conservatory out of the garden to the Stand Wood above. A rediscovered Greek altar marks the top of this new walk.

Soon the *'clear stream, brought with much care from a distance of two miles from the East Moor makes its first appearance; the purest water, and a course so natural, that the walk appears to be made for it, not it for the walk'*. (6th Duke's Handbook)

In about 300 yards you reach the Cascade House.

"Little Trout" stream

Steps to the south-east of the Old Conservatory Garden

31

THE AZALEA DELL
AND THE RAVINE

Rhododendrons and azaleas (now considered to be the same genus) grow well at Chatsworth as the soil and conditions suit all but the tender varieties. This part of the garden is devoted to them and the Dell is planted with a solid mass of azaleas: Ghent, double Ghent, and A. *ponticum* (now *Rhododendron luteum*). Towards the end of May it is a goodly sight from the path above, and on a windless day the smell of these sweet-scented shrubs is unforgettable. The Ghent varieties are slightly later than the rest and have a particularly good smell. These deciduous azaleas do double duty as they colour brilliantly in the autumn. The south-facing bank of the Ravine is a wall of *Rhododendron ponticum*; not a plant to be encouraged all over the garden because of its rampant and invasive habit, but on this steep bank it is impressive and worth keeping as a reminder of Victorian times when it was fashionable and something of a novelty.

Evelyn, wife of the 9th Duke of Devonshire, who lived at Chatsworth from 1907 to 1938, paid great attention to this part of the garden and made massive plantings of spring flowers. The 'wild garden' was high fashion then and this was an ideal place for such a scheme. During the war of 1939-45 it was neglected and there is little left of her designs for her favourite part of the garden.

The bright yellow *Lysichiton americanus* (skunk cabbage) grows in the stream which runs from the Grotto Pond and disappears under the Azalea Dell. The earliest snowdrops are on the south-facing bank, and so is the sweet-scented *Mahonia bealei* and various rhododendron hybrids which have reached maturity. A planting of *Kalmia latifolia* is on the right of the steep track just before you join the main path at the Grotto Pond.

The skunk cabbage (*Lysichiton americanus*)

THE CANAL POND AND THE EMPEROR FOUNTAIN

The canal and the fountain are two of the most dominant features of the garden. Although the fountain you now see was Paxton's creation (see below), a Great Fountain was part of the 1st Duke's scheme when he rebuilt the Elizabethan house in classical style. The Canal Pond was dug in 1702. Until then there was a hill to the south, obscuring the view down the valley. Daniel Defoe came to Chatsworth before this radical change of the landscape had been made and when he returned a few years later he could not believe his eyes when he saw the sheet of water 314 yards long.

'The Duke . . . has removed a great mountain that stood in the way', he wrote, 'I was perfectly confounded . . . for I had lost the hill, and found a new country in view'.

It remained unaltered for 140 years till 1843 when it became known that Czar Nicholas, Emperor of Russia, might visit Chatsworth during his stay in England the following year. The 6th Duke was a friend of the Emperor and had seen the great fountain at Peterhof when he stayed at the Imperial Palace for the coronation in 1826. The idea of welcoming the Czar at Chatsworth with an even higher fountain appealed to the Duke, so Paxton set to work on a job after his own heart where his talent for engineering had full play.

34

The abundant supply of water on the hill above the garden made endless possibilities of using it for displays of gravity-fed waterworks but it had to be stored and harnessed to its work. Paxton started his survey to determine the levels in December 1843. A conduit 2½ miles long was dug across the moor to drain water into the new reservoir 350 feet above the house. The digging of this 8-acre lake was a major task. 100,000 cubic yards of earth were moved by man- and horse-power and the banks were lined with stone. Its average depth was seven feet. *'I walked up with Paxton to see the new reservoir, half frightened by the immense work'* wrote the Duke in his diary.

The Emperor Fountain
c. 1850. Lithograph by
J. C. Bourne

Between 1893 and 1936 electricity was generated for Chatsworth by three water turbines using the enormous pressure of the Emperor main. In 1988 a new turbine was installed and this now generates about a third of all the electricity the house needs.

Portrait head, bronze, of
Dame Elisabeth Frink by
Angela Conner, 1992

The work progressed at speed, continuing at night by the light of flares, and in six months it was finished. Alas, the Czar never came to Chatsworth, but the Emperor Fountain was named after him and is a splendid sight to this day. It is on record as having reached the height of 296 feet.

The limes were already big enough for Dr. Johnson to walk under when he visited the 5th Duke and Georgiana in 1784. The grassy mound at the south-west end of the canal is the ice-house, in use till the 1920s. As the canal is only two feet deep it makes a perfect ice rink and skating was very popular here with the girls of Penrhos College during the last war (above).

Dame Elisabeth
Frink and the
Duchess of
Devonshire at the
unveiling of the War
Horse, April 1992

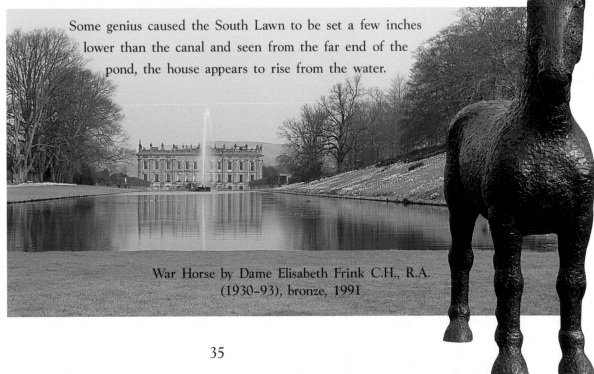

Some genius caused the South Lawn to be set a few inches lower than the canal and seen from the far end of the pond, the house appears to rise from the water.

War Horse by Dame Elisabeth Frink C.H., R.A.
(1930–93), bronze, 1991

THE SOUTH LAWN

The South Lawn (which is private) is the oldest surviving flat terrace dating from the time of the Elizabethan house. The containing wall to the west is of the same date.

The water from the base of the Cascade is piped to the Sea-horse Fountain. The resulting pressure from the 50 foot drop provides the force for the display here. The water disappears again, descends 30 feet to the pond in the West Garden to work the Tulip Fountain, whence it is piped under the garden wall into the river Derwent.

Inset: The Sea-horse Fountain

Triton and the Sea-horses were carved by Caius Gabriel Cibber (1630-1700). Three hundred years of buffeting by weather and water have had a sad effect on the stone, but the horses are still full of life and movement. Cibber worked here for four years (1688-91) but most of his outdoor statuary was replaced in the 19th century, so this example of his work is all the more precious. In the lime hedge are eight statues and two vases which were *'worked for me by Francesco Bienaimé at Carrara, of hard marble of that place, that appears to defy the climate of the Peak, and to resist all incipient vegetation on its surface. I think them a great addition; the eye reposes with pleasure on these classic forms'*. (6th Duke's *Handbook*, 1844.)

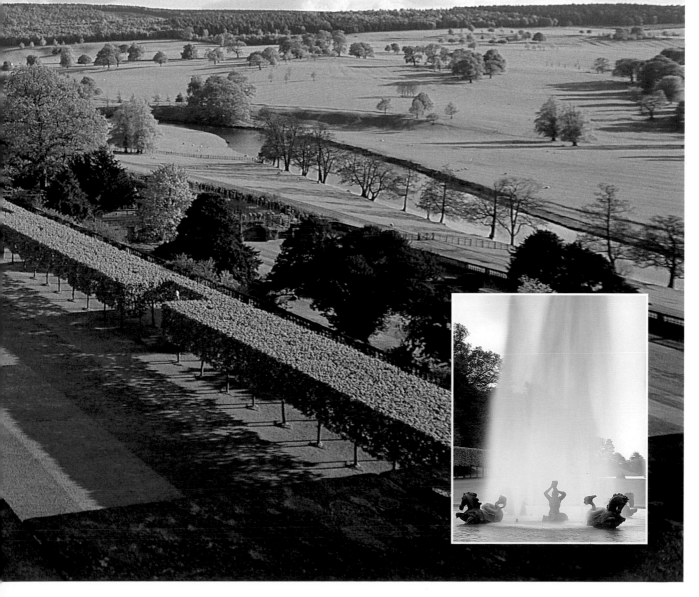

When I first knew the South Lawn in the 1940s there were eight raised beds between the statues. They were surrounded by tufa rock and contained thin pink 'Poulsen' roses. We thought them out of scale and too mean for their grand situation so, in 1952, we replaced them with double rows of pleached red-twigged limes (*Tilia platyphyllos* 'Rubra'). Like all new planting in a place of such size and importance they looked ridiculous for years.

Wyatville's rather ponderous stone stairs (1837) which he copied from Chiswick House, replaced Talman's simpler and more delicate curved flights and Tijou's wrought-iron balustrade.

In 1950 all the plate-glass windows on the South Front were replaced with composite frames (24 panes on the first floor, 28 on the second), restoring their original appearance. Since the 18th century the window frames on the South and West Fronts have been gilded with real gold leaf, which has to be renewed about every 30 years.

The South Lawn looking south from the bronze copy by Sir Francis Chantrey of Canova's *Endymion* towards the Canal Pond

The South Terrace and Steps

Statue in Carrara marble of the *Apollo Belvedere*, after the Antique, by Francesco Bienaimé 1841

Their wooden supports, much bigger than the limes themselves, and the wires they were to be trained along, looked like pylons. It took about fifteen years in this exposed situation for the limes to make anything approaching the effect that was planned. Now, after more than forty years, they make two solid green lines twelve feet high and eighteen feet wide, leading the eye to the house from the canal. They are clipped once a year, at the end of July.

The massive stone window boxes are filled with 400 wallflowers in the spring followed by pelargonium 'Vera Dillon' in the summer. There is a large patch of thyme in the grass near the pond, and many of the other wild flowers seen on the Salisbury Lawns thrive here.

In the late 19th century there were flower beds on the east bank. They were shaped like swagged pelmets and the outlines are clearly visible in a dry summer. Mulleins (*Verbascum*) seed themselves freely in the broad paths of spar gravel.

THE RING POND
AND SERPENTINE HEDGE

The Ring Pond looking east

The rocks in the middle of the Ring Pond support an ancient lead duck (1693), moved there from a pond which has been filled in. Water spouts from its beak as

The 12 stone busts on tapering columns originally decorated William Kent's Exedra in the garden at Chiswick and were brought here c. 1930. The statue of the man carrying a goat at the top of the beech avenue came from the garden at Devonshire House in Piccadilly, London.

it did in its old home, which of course was called the Sick Duck Pond. The huge pipe which is clearly visible underwater is the feeder pipe for the Emperor Fountain.

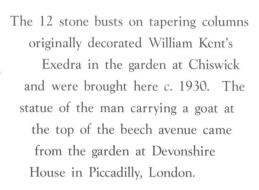

39

The serpentine hedge of beech (*Fagus sylvatica*) was planted in 1953. The reason for its existence is that we thought the bronze head of the 6th Duke at the far (south) end deserved an approach of importance. In his *Handbook* (1845) the Duke describes it thus ". . . *the column composed of four circular blocks of marble is indeed most interesting, having been part of the temple of Minerva Sunias: they were brought home by Sir Augustus Clifford: and he had not robbed the shrine, for they had already been rolled down to the sea-beach, where sand and waves would soon have concealed them. The bust was executed by Campbell without any order, and for twenty years had encumbered his studio; at last I have relieved him of it, and it is to encounter the storms of the Peak in this exposed situation. But certainly no bust ever had so grand a pedestal'.*

We decided on a serpentine design for the walk after seeing the 'crinkle crankle' wall at Hopton Hall near Wirksworth. A wall was out of the question here so we used beech to make the same effect. Like the limes on the South Lawn it looked hopelessly out of scale when it was planted at 18 inches high and twenty years passed before it began to look right. In the gale of 1962 five forest trees fell across it and the 6th Duke's head crashed from its column in a sorry mess of branches. It was undamaged. The crushed beeches were replaced and a year later it was impossible to see the chaos caused by the hurricane. The hedge has now reached its required height. It is clipped once a year, in August.

THE COTTAGE GARDEN

The exhibit of the Cheshire Women's Institutes at the Chelsea Flower Show in 1988 was the inspiration for the Cottage Garden. We thought that something on that scale would be a welcome addition here. We have added 'furniture' on two levels. There is a front garden of flower beds bordered by box, which leads to a kitchen/dining room. This has a dining table, chairs and a sofa constructed of rustic poles with yew and privet planted at each leg and clipped to their shapes. There is a fireplace which has a surround of golden privet; the flames are geraniums and the ashes are the grey leaves of artemisia.

Dining table, chairs and sofa

The front garden

Entrance to the Vegetable Garden

A flight of yew stairs goes up to the bedroom. The four-poster bed covered by the large-leaved ivy *Hedera Canariensis Ravensholt*, yew bedside tables and ivy 'Tiffany' lamps (grown over the frames of children's umbrellas), a chaise-longue of forsythia at the foot of the bed, a privet dressing table, ivy mirror, yew chair and camomile carpet complete the bedroom furniture. The seat of the chair is thyme. The planting of the bedspread, to look like chintz, is changed each year.

42

The Cottage has its own vegetable garden (42' x 28') at the back, surrounded by an oak fence. The oak is from blown trees in the park. The posts are riven by an axe down the grain in the way fencing is often portrayed in old pictures. A chicken run with Light Sussex hens is next to this plot. It never ceases to amaze me that such a quantity and variety of vegetables can come out of such a small space and I believe it has encouraged some people to start growing their own produce.

THE KITCHEN GARDEN

The 11 acre kitchen garden half a mile away in the park was abandoned in 1946. Thereafter a few vegetables were grown in what is now a more ambitious kitchen garden. This ground was originally paddocks where the carriage horses were turned out, being near to the stables. The greenhouses were already there, but it was a dreary, featureless patch when we decided to improve it. We thought the new enthusiasm for growing vegetables and fruit merited an investment to make the place more interesting and open for all to see. It was re-designed during the winters of 1991/2 and 1992/3. The necessary drains were laid, raised beds were built from old bricks and some new paths were bordered by railway sleepers. Iron arches to support apples and runner beans were erected and a grand compost container was built of brick. A quantity of top soil was imported. In 1993 the outdoor frames were renewed. The fruit cage is necessary to keep out pheasants, small birds and grey squirrels. All the young leaves of the new fruit trees trained on the south-facing stone wall were eaten by its resident mice, so it had to be pointed with cement. Asparagus, sea kale and globe artichokes as well as decorative vegetables like the brilliant red rhubarb chard and gourds are grown.

The house is now supplied with vegetables grown here and the Carriage House Restaurant takes lettuces and other salads. The surplus is sold at the Potting Shed and the Farm Shop. Herbs are planted in squares along the length of the central path and the big vegetable beds are bordered with parsley and the 'alpine' strawberries *Baron Solemacher* and *Alexandria*. Beyond a beech hedge at the lower part of the garden is a small orchard with arable field wild flowers corn-cockle, corn-marigold, corn-flower, poppy and wild pansy. Above the entrance to the new kitchen garden is the Golden Grove, planted with shrubs and trees of that colour given to us to mark our Golden Wedding in 1991.

I believe a garden the size of Chatsworth needs movement as well as plants, trees and buildings. The water in all its facets – fountains, cascade and ponds – goes a long way towards adding this variety. The more timid of the wild creatures are seldom seen in the daytime but unusual poultry are at large round the greenhouses as well as waterfowl on the ponds. However, the garden was made for people to look at and walk in and I hope the readers of this guidebook will look and walk and enjoy the garden at Chatsworth.

Deborah Devonshire

CHATSWORTH GARDEN
Five Centuries of Change

The Elizabethan Garden

The earliest reference to a garden at Chatsworth is in a letter written by Bess of Hardwick and dated 8th March 1560, eight years after she and her second husband Sir William Cavendish had begun to build the first house there:-

I would have the letell garden weche ys by the newe howse made a garden thys yere. I care not wether you bestow any grate cost thereof; but to sowe yt with al kynde of earbes and flowres, and some pece of yt with malos. I have sende you by thys carerer 3 bundeles of garden sedes all wreten with Willem Marchyngton's hande; and by the next you shall know how to youse them yn every pynte.

A page showing Chatsworth from the *Survey* by William Senior of the estates of the Earl of Devonshire, 1617, watercolour on vellum

The house, garden and park are shown much as Sir William Cavendish and Bess of Hardwick left them.

The earliest published account of the garden is by Thomas Hobbes in his poem *De Mirabilibus Pecci*, written *c.* 1627 and first published in 1636. The English translation includes the lines:-

Behind, a pleasant Garden does appear;
Where the rich earth, breaths odours everywhere,
Where in the midst of Woods, the fruitful Tree
Bears without prune-hook, seeming now as free.
Where by the thickleav'd roof the Walls are made
Spite of the Sun were all his beams display'd,
More cool than the fam'd Virgil's Beechen shade.

Hobbes goes on to describe the fountains, fed from lead pipes:-

The Water that from native cliffs had source
Once free and unconfin'd, throughout it's course,
By it's own Country Metal is led on
Captive to Rocks of Artificial stone.
There buried deep, it's streams it doubly throws
Into two circling Channels as it goes,
Through thousand cranies, which by art it does
Then girds the Rock with many a hollow vain,
Frighting all under with surprising rain,
Thence turning it a Marble font does store,
Until it's lofty brims can hold no more.

(from Thomas Hobbes *De Mirabilibus Pecci; being the Wonders of the Peak*. 5th ed. London, 1683)

Half a century later, Charles Cotton writes of Chatsworth in his *Wonders of the Peake* (London, 1681):-

To view from hence the glittering Pile above,
(Which must at once Wonder create and love)
Environ'd round with natures Shames, and Ills,
Black Heaths, wild Rocks, bleak Craggs, and naked Hills,
And the whole Prospect so inform, and rude,
Who is it, but must presently conclude?
That this is Paradise, which seated stands
In midst of Desarts, and of barren Sands.
So a bright Diamond would look, if set
In a vile socket of ignoble Jet . . .

The First Duke's Garden

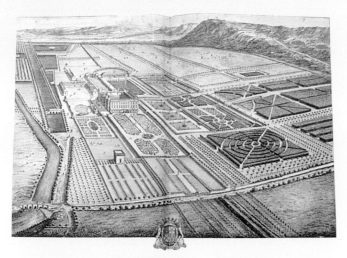

Chatsworth in September 1699, engraved by Jan Kip
after a drawing by Leendert Knyff

In 1690 George London and Henry Wise were engaged, first to lay out the West Parterre and later (1694) the South or Great Parterre, which measured 473 x 227 feet. London and Wise, the country's leading garden makers and designers at the time, were paid £500 for the Great Parterre and also supplied a large number of trees and shrubs from their 100-acre nursery at Brompton Park, as the entries from the Chatsworth account books show:–

20th June 1690	Mr. London's man for Greens and other trees for the new garden at Chatsworth	£8 18s 0d
28th Sept 1697	Mr. Wise for 220 Yews, Hollys & Juniper	£50 0s 0d
22nd July 1698	Mr. Wise for 50 Orange trees, 12 Laurustinus, 20 Yews & 20 Swedish Junipers	£160 0s 0d
24th March 1698	Mr. Wise for 26 Apricotts & 14 Peach trees & 60 Swedish Junipers for Chatsworth	£24 3s 0d

Celia Fiennes, writing her diary in 1696, describes the view that she had of the 1st Duke's Garden from the hilltop to the east:–

'The Duke's house Lyes just at ye foote of this steepe hill which is like a precipice just at ye Last, notwithstanding the Dukes house stands on a little riseing ground from ye River Derwent which runns all along ye front of ye house, and by a Little fall made in ye water which makes a pretty Murmurring noise. Before ye gate there is a Large parke and Severall ffine Gardens one without another with Gravell walkes and and Squairs of Grass with stone statues in them, and in ye middle of Each Garden is a Large ffountaine full of Images, sea gods and Dolphins and sea horses which are full of pipes which spout out water in the bason and spouts all about the Gardens. 3 gardens just round the house. Out of two of ye Gardens you ascend by Severall Stepps into other Gardens which have some Gravell walks and squares Like ye other with Statues and Images in the bason. There is one bason in the Middle of one Garden thats very Large and by sluces besides the Images Severall pipes plays out ye water - about 30 Large and small pipes altogether, some fflush it up that it ffrothes Like snow. There is one Garden full of stone and brass statues. So the Gardens Lyes one above another which makes the prospect very fine. Above these gardens is an ascent of 5 or 6 stepps up to green walk and groves of firrs and a wilderness and Close arbours and shady walks. On each end of one Walke stands two piramidies full of pipes spouting water that runns down one of them – runns on brass hollow work which looks like rocks and hollow stones . . . .

(from *Through England on a Side Saddle in the Time of William and Mary, being the diary of Celia Fiennes.* **London, 1888; new illustrated edition 1982.**)

Bird's-eye view of Chatsworth
from the south-east *c.* 1707

Sixty years after Celia Fiennes' visit the 4th Duke engaged Lancelot 'Capability' Brown to redesign the garden and park in the spirit of the new 'landscape' movement and the accounts show the type of work that was carried out, as much civil engineering as gardening:–

9th March 1758	Thos. Gould & Partners for raising the new pondhead with earth & clay, & filling ye old pond	£13 5s 0d
31st July 1761	Sundry labourers leveling draining & cleaning where the fences stood in ye grounds now in ye New Parke	£27 12s 6d
19th July 1760 to 21st Nov. 1761	To Mr. Melican, as by his receipts, upon Mr. Brown's account	£900 0s 0d

(Michael Melican, or Milliken, acted as Lancelot Brown's foreman at Chatsworth until 1765).

19th Dec. 1761	John Shaw for 6500 nails for Park Palings	£1 11s 7d
4th Apr. 1762	Frances Harrison widow removeing earth with her cart and horses	£14 4s 0d
25th Apr. 1762	John Haworth for 20 quarter hayseeds delivered to sow the New laid down grounds	£5 10s 0d
29th June 1763	Wm. Miller & Thos. Bland walling ye Sunke Fence near ye Canal	£12 19s 0d

Chatsworth from the south west.
Engraving by M. A. Rooker after Paul Sandby, 1775

Horace Walpole visited Chatsworth in 1760 and in a letter to George Montagu (1st September 1760) expressed his misgivings about the 4th Duke's plans:–

I went with the Straffords to Chatsworth, and stayed there four days . . . Would you believe that nothing was ever better humoured than the ancient Grace? [widow of the 3rd Duke]. She stayed every evening till it was dark in the skittle-ground, keeping the score . . . I never was more disappointed than at Chatsworth, which, ever since I was born, I have condemned. It is a glorious situation; the vale rich in corn and verdure, vast woods hang down the hills, which are green to the top, and the immense rocks only serve to dignify the prospect. The river runs before the door, and serpentises more than you can conceive in the vale. The Duke is widening it, and will make it the middle of his park; but I don't approve an idea they are going to execute, of a fine bridge with statues under a noble cliff. If they will have a bridge (which by the way will crowd the scene), it should be composed of rude fragments, such as the giant of the Peak would step upon, that he might not be wet-shod . . . The great jet d'eau I like, nor would I remove it; whatever is magnificent of the kind in the time it was done, I would retain, else all gardens and houses wear a tiresome resemblance. I except that absurdity of a cascade tumbling down marble steps, which reduces the steps to be of no use at all.

(from *The Letters of Horace Walpole*, edited by Peter Cunningham, Vol.3. London, 1891).

Eight years later Walpole visited Chatsworth again and revised his opinion:–

Chatsworth in Derbyshire. Duke of Devonshire's; I had seen it before, but it is much improved by the late Duke, many foolish waterworks being taken away, oaks and rocks taken into the garden, & a magnificent bridge built.

(from *Horace Walpole's journals of visits to country seats &c* Walpole Society, vol. 16, 1927-8).

The Sixth Duke's Garden & Joseph Paxton

Paxton was appointed Head Gardener at Chatsworth in 1826 at the age of 23, and his description of his first morning there is quoted by the 6th Duke in the *Handbook of Chatsworth and Hardwick* (London, 1845):–

I left London by the Comet coach to Chesterfield, arrived at Chatsworth at half past four o'clock in the morning of the ninth of May, 1826. As no person was to be seen at that early hour, I got over the greenhouse gate by the old covered way, explored the pleasure-grounds, and looked around the outside of the house. I then went down to the kitchen-gardens, scaled the outside wall, and saw the whole of the place, set the men to work there at six o'clock; then returned to Chatsworth, and got Thomas Weldon to play me the water-works, and afterwards went to breakfast with poor dear Mrs. Gregory and her niece: the latter fell in love with me, and I with her, and thus completed my first morning's work at Chatsworth before nine o'clock.

Joseph Paxton
(1803–65) by Henry Briggs

The 6th Duke goes on to describe the state of the gardens at the time:–

At the kitchen-garden he (Paxton) found four pine-houses, bad; two vineries, which contained eight bunches of grapes; two good peach houses, and a few cucumber frames. There were no houses at all for plants, and there was nowhere a plant of later introduction than about the year 1800. There were eight rhododendrons, and not one camellia. He married Miss Sarah Bown in 1827. In a very short time a great change appeared in pleasure-ground and garden: vegetables, of which there had been none, fruit in perfection, and flowers. The twelve men with brooms in their hands on the lawn began to sweep, the labourers to work with activity.

John Claudius Loudon (1783-1843) was often a severe critic of both Paxton and Chatsworth. He wrote in the *Gardener's Magazine* (vol. 7, 1831), of which he was the editor:–

Chatsworth has always appeared to us an unsatisfactory place. The house is not situated on a platform of adequate size; and there is great awkwardness in the approach proceeding abruptly up hill . . . the waterworks, though good in themselves, are scattered about the grounds in such a way, that, while they interfere *everywhere with the natural beauties of the place, they no where combine in forming one grand artificial effect. They want concentration.*

Loudon goes on to criticize the new flower-gardens (*in a highly enriched architectural taste*), the use of gravel for the walks, the introduction of flowers into the kitchen-garden (*we would as soon introduce a plot of cabbages in the newly formed parterre at the house*), and Paxton's use of wood for his new greenhouses. Eight years later, however, he had completely changed his opinion. In the *Gardener's Magazine* for 1839 he wrote:–

The Duke of Devonshire has stated to us that he owed his taste in botany and gardening entirely to Mr. Paxton. There are but few persons in the present day whose talents and exertions have conferred more service on the science of botany and gardening than the gentleman to whom the above compliment is paid. A few years only have transpired since Chatsworth, as far as gardening was concerned, was below mediocrity. Its noble owner bestowed neither money nor patronage in advancing the art; in fact he had no taste for gardening. Now he is its best and most influential friend.

When Loudon died in 1843 it was Paxton who helped to raise financial aid for his widow.

Of Paxton's achievements at Chatsworth, the colossal scale of his rockeries and of the Great Conservatory caused the most astonishment at the time. Mrs. S.C. Hall wrote in 1851:–

The most striking and original of the walks is that which leads through mimic Alpine scenery to the great conservatory; here Art has been most triumphant; the rocks which have all been brought hither are so skilfully combined, so richly clad in mosses, so luxuriantly covered with heather, so judiciously based with ferns and water-plants, that you move among, or beside, them, in rare delight at the sudden change which transports you from trim parterres to the utmost wildness of natural beauty. From these again you pass into a garden, in the centre of which is the conservatory, always renowned, but now more than ever, as the prototype of the famous Palace of Glass [the Crystal Palace], which, in this Annus Mirabilis, received under its roof six millions of the people of all nations, tongues, and creeds. The conservatory at Chatsworth . . . is filled with the rarest Exotics from all parts of the globe - from 'farthest Ind', from China, from the Himalayas, from Mexico; here you see the rich banana, Eschol's grape, hanging in ripe profusion beneath the shadow of immense paper-like leaves; the feathery cocoa-palm, with its head peering almost to the lofty arched roof; the far-famed silk cotton-tree, supplying a sheet of cream-coloured blossoms, at a season when all outward vegetable gaiety is on the wane; the singular milk-tree of the Caraccas; the fragrant cinnamon and cassia - with thousands of other rare and little known species of both flowers and fruits.

(from *A day at Chatsworth* **by Mrs. S. C. Hall.** *The Art-Journal* **1851).**

The fame of the garden at Chatsworth was not confined to this country. In 1854 Charles de Saint-Amant, Governor of the Tuileries in Paris, wrote a book about Chatsworth he called *Le Second Versailles*, much of which was devoted to the park and garden:–

Returning to our parallel between Versailles and Chatsworth, let's walk for a while from one greensward to the next. Do they only remind you of that wretched lawn at Versailles, which one is so happy to trample over blindfold? Sparse and impoverished at any season, can it dare compare itself with these broad expanses of turf and flowering moss, softer and more gentle to the tread than swansdown? We have never found such fitted carpets of turf as those in English parks. Nature, generally so beautiful when left to herself, nowhere equals these works where the labours of art are on hand to add to her value, without detracting in any way from her more primitive qualities. And as we have already said, it is impossible for intimate affinities not to exist between the trees and the grass of this park, when you admire the sympathetic way they lend each other mutual support. Neither the roots nor the shade of the former encroaches in any way on what lives at their feet. It is right to add that hands – invisible but many and attentive – watch over everything and control each element's share. The vegetation, which seems to be neither hampered nor constrained, and which above all isn't mutilated like the tree-covered walks of Versailles, so stiff in their wall-like uniformity, is nonetheless subject to constant attention, and in every season. It is only plucked, as it were, of unwanted hair, so as to hide in a coquettish way and for as long as possible the ravages of time; and a watch is kept, too, to safeguard it against accidents and to forestall diseases. Let's never forget that all this goes on under a sky rarely without clouds and where the miserly rays of sunshine are often veiled by the densest fogs. As to smoke, you will see there is no need to speak of it at Chatsworth . . .

On all sides you see only flower beds, baskets of flowers, cradles and bowers of climbing plants, varied and many-flowered shrubs, coverings so dense as to make you believe in the dangers of an English sun. And these living hedges of rose bushes, sparkling with Lilliputian flowers, which without any break of continuity flank paths the ends of which are never seen!

(*Le Second Versailles* **Paris, 1854. Translated from the French.)**

The *Victoria Regia* Lily House in the former Kitchen Garden, c. 1900